THE SESAME STREET QUESTION AND ANSWER BOOK ABOUT ANIMALS

by RAE PAIGE

illustrated by JEAN ZALLINGER

Featuring Jim Henson's Sesame Street Muppets

A SESAME STREET/A GOLDEN BOOK
Published by Western Publishing Company, Inc.
in conjunction with Children's Television Workshop.

Consultants

George Fichter
Naturalist and Biologist

David Parsons
Chief Exhibit Preparator
Peabody Museum, Yale University

Library of Congress Catalog Card Number: 81-84709
ISBN 0-307-15816-0/ISBN 0-307-65816-3 (lib. bdg.)
B C D E F G H I J

TABLE OF CONTENTS

THE SESAME STREET QUESTION AND ANSWER BOOK ABOUT ANIMALS

What Animals Lay Eggs?

Many animals—
not just birds—lay eggs.
Turtles, frogs,
some snakes, fishes, bees,
ants, snails, platypuses,
alligators and crocodiles are
just a few of the
many animals that lay eggs.
Even dinosaurs
came from eggs.

Are all eggs white?

No. Many are naturally blue, pink, green, brown, and speckled brown, gray and black. And then there are Easter eggs!

Emperor penguins have a special way of taking care of their eggs. After the mother lays the egg, the father keeps it warm in a fold of skin just above his feet.

What is the smallest egg?

The smallest egg in the world is the hummingbird egg. It's about the size of a raisin.

What is the biggest egg?

The biggest egg in the world is the ostrich egg. It's as big as a large grapefruit.

"Hey, Bert. How do chickens lay their eggs inside those little cardboard egg cartons?"

"They don't, Ernie. Chickens lay their eggs in nests. Farmers gather the eggs and put them in cartons."

11

What Are Baby Animals Called?

"Hmm. It says in this book a baby owl is called an owlet. What do we call a baby grouch, Oscar?"

"A grouchlet, of course."

piglet

chicks

calves

cubs

pups

joey

kitten

foal

13

What Do Baby Animals Look Like?

Some babies look like
their parents, only smaller.

tigers

dolphins

lions

14

dogs

zebras

swans

Some babies don't look like
their parents at all.

butterfly

frog

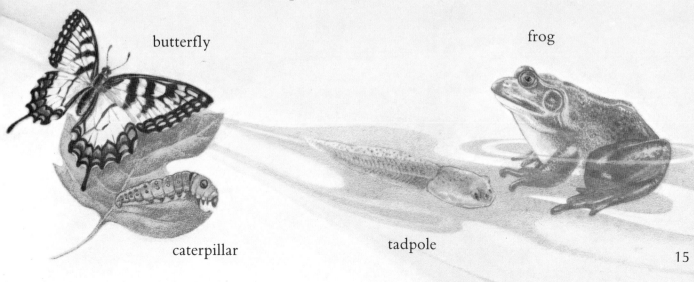

caterpillar

tadpole

15

How Do Parents Carry Their Babies?

Parents carry their babies around in many different ways.

A baby kangaroo lives in its mother's pouch for about six months.

A monkey parent can swing through the trees with a baby monkey hanging onto its neck.

A beaver parent sometimes carries its baby cradled in its arms.

16

Young opossums
hold on to their mother's
fur as she walks.

A father seahorse carries
seahorse eggs in a pouch
until the eggs hatch.

Human babies sometimes ride
on their parent's back, too.

A mother cat
sometimes carries her kitten
by the scruff of the neck.

A baby hippopotamus
rides on its mother's back
in the water.

True or False?

Raccoons roast their corn before they eat it.
True or false?

FALSE. But they do sometimes dunk their
food in water before they eat it.

Penguins like to go sledding.
True or false?

TRUE. They slide down
snowy hills
on their stomachs.

18

Elephants wear hats. True or false?

TRUE. Elephants sometimes make hats of wet grass and mud to keep the hot sun off their heads.

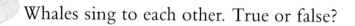

Whales sing to each other. True or false?

TRUE. They make sounds like singing which seem to "tell" things to other whales.

Bulls charge at a red cape because they hate red. True or false?

FALSE. Bulls are color-blind and can't tell red from any other color. Bulls charge at a cape waving in front of them because of its movement, not its color.

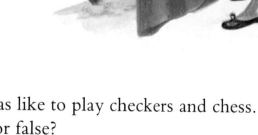

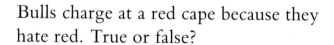

Gorillas like to play checkers and chess. True or false?

FALSE. But baby gorillas play games very much like follow the leader and king of the mountain.

What's the Difference?

...between a tiger and a leopard?
A tiger has stripes and
a leopard has spots.

...between a horse and a zebra?
The zebra is the one with the stripes.

20

...between a horse and a donkey?
The donkey is the one with the long ears.

...between a camel and a dromedary?
None. A dromedary is a kind of camel—
the kind with only one hump.

...between a groundhog and a woodchuck?
Nothing. Those are two names for the same animal.

Who Lives in the Sea?

Many animals live underwater.

seahorse

lobster

clam

sponge

starfish

squid

dolphin

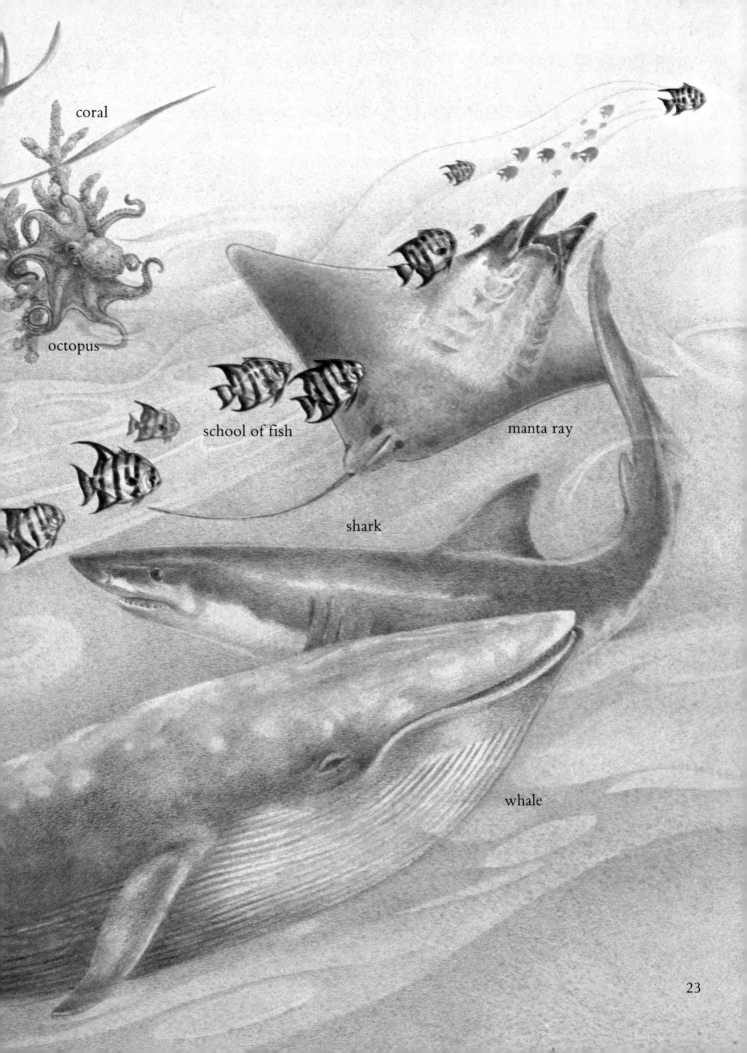

coral

octopus

school of fish

manta ray

shark

whale

23

Who's Winning?

These animals are all crawling, running, hopping, jumping, flying, galloping or swimming as fast as they can. Who do you think will win the race?

hawk
35 mph (miles per hour)

elephant
25 mph

giraffe
32 mph

reindeer
32 mph

race horse
47 mph

person
27 mph

greyhound
39 mph

cat
30 mph

snail
1½ miles per week

rabbit
35 mph

penguin
30 mph

blue whale
25 mph

dolphin
37 mph

24

spine-tailed swift
100 mph

cheetah
70 mph

sailfish
65 mph

25

Bats and...

"Greetings! I am the Count. Let me introduce you to my wonderful, beautiful bats!"

Bats are the only animals besides birds and insects that can fly. Most bats fly at night and sleep all day, hanging by their feet in caves or other dark places.

How do bats fly at night without bumping into things?
Bats have a special kind of hearing which helps them sense where things are, even when they can't see them.

Are bats really blind?
No. Many people think that bats are blind, but bats really have good eyesight.

...Cats

"Here, kitty, kitty, kitty! I like pussycats because they have soft fur just like mine. Ya."

How can you tell if a cat is scared?
When a cat is frightened, it hisses, arches its back, and puffs up its fur.

Why do cats lick themselves?
To get clean. Cats lick themselves all over with their scratchy tongues to clean their fur. They wash their faces and their ears by licking their paws and using them as washcloths.

How do cats climb trees?
By digging their claws into the bark of the tree. Cats also use their claws as weapons.

Is it true that cats have nine lives?
No. People just say that because cats have a knack for getting out of danger.

Can cats see in the dark?
Cats are able to see in very dim light but not in complete darkness.

27

Big Bird's Bird Questions

"A bird is an animal with feathers, two wings, two legs, a beak, and no teeth. Isn't he adorable?"

HOME TWEET HOME

Can all birds fly?
No. Penguins and ostriches and some other birds can't fly because their wings are too small.

Are bald eagles really bald?

No. They just look that way from a distance because the feathers on their heads are a very light color.

Why do woodpeckers peck on trees?

They eat the little insects that live in the bark.

Why don't woodpeckers get headaches when they peck on trees?

Because they have very hard bills and special padding in their heads.

"Hey, Ern, why do hummingbirds hum?"

"Because they don't know the words, Bert?"

"No, Ernie. When hummingbirds fly, their wings beat very fast and make a humming sound."

29

Oscar's Yucchy Questions

What does a camel do when it's grouchy?
It spits.

Why do pigs roll around in the mud?
To keep cool.

Do goats eat tin cans?
No, but they chew on them because they like the taste of the glue that holds the labels on the cans.

What does a skunk do when it's afraid?
It sprays a stinky mist toward its enemy.

How can you get rid of skunk smell?
Scrub anything skunky with tomato juice, soap, and water.

"Hey! Who wants to get rid of it?"

How Many?

"Greetings! Can you tell me how many?"

How many feet does a snail have?
One. One foot.

How many arms does an octopus have?
Eight. Eight arms!

How many arms does a starfish have?
Five. Five arms.

How many legs does a spider have?
Eight. Eight legs.

How many legs does a ladybug have?
Six. Six legs!

How many legs does a centipede have?
Most centipedes have 35 pairs of legs,
or 70 legs in all. Seventy legs!

How many heads does a two-headed monster have?
Two. Two heads!

31

Small World

"Here are some of the smallest animals in the world."

DWARF PYGMY GOBY FISH
It's tinier than a thimble.

BEE HUMMINGBIRD
It's as small as a walnut.

BUMBLEBEE BAT
Its body is as small
as a peach pit.

PYGMY SHREW
It would fit in the palm
of a small child's hand.

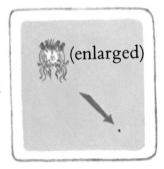

(enlarged)

ITCHMITE
The itchmite is so small
that you can't see it.

Big News

"Here's some big news."

What is the biggest animal of all?
The blue whale. It weighs as much as a locomotive. It's the biggest animal that has ever lived, even bigger than a dinosaur!

What's the biggest cat?
The biggest member of the cat family is the tiger. A tiger grows to be more than ten feet long from the tip of its nose to the tip of its tail. It weighs as much as four grownups.

What is the biggest land animal?
The African elephant. It weighs as much as two cars.

What is the biggest bird?
The ostrich is the biggest bird in the world. It's as tall as a very big bear.

What's For Dinner?

Some snakes can unhinge their jaw to swallow an egg larger than the width of their body.

"What do Cookie Monsters really eat? Cuppy cakes. (And fruits and vegetables, and cheese and meat.)"

Pelicans catch fish for dinner.

An anteater sticks out his long tongue to lick up ants and other insects.

Cows and horses eat grass.

Giraffes eat leaves from the tiptops of acacia trees.

Flamingoes eat with their heads upside-down. They filter mud with their beaks to find tiny bugs

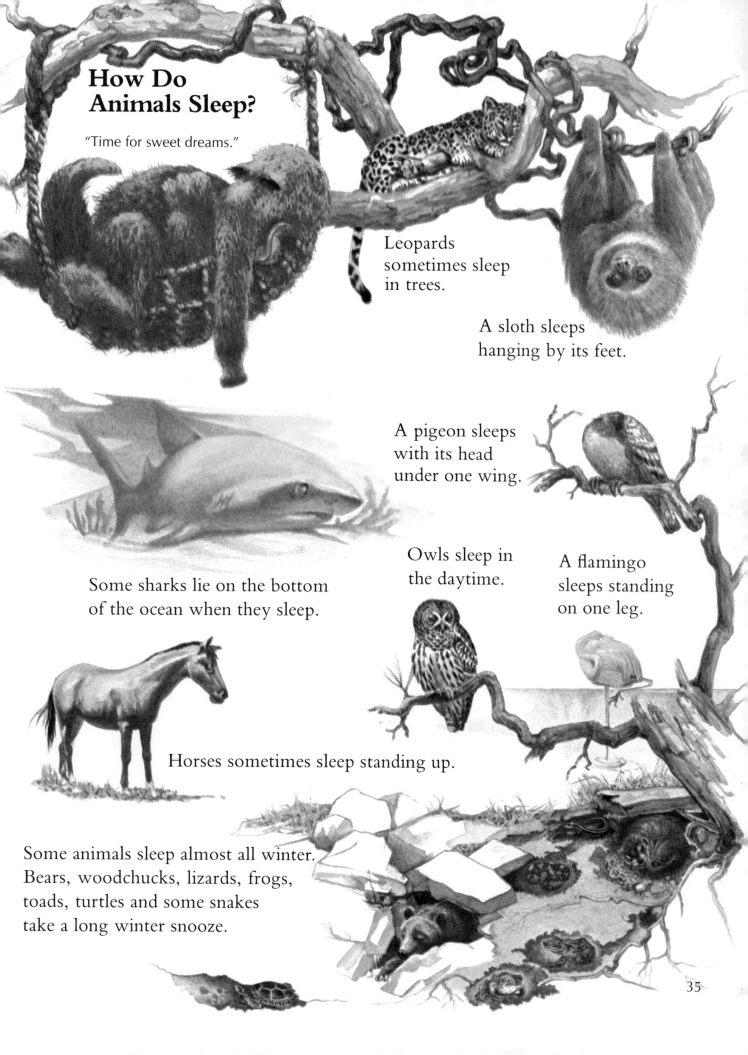

How Do Animals Sleep?

"Time for sweet dreams."

Leopards
sometimes sleep
in trees.

A sloth sleeps
hanging by its feet.

A pigeon sleeps
with its head
under one wing.

Some sharks lie on the bottom
of the ocean when they sleep.

Owls sleep in
the daytime.

A flamingo
sleeps standing
on one leg.

Horses sometimes sleep standing up.

Some animals sleep almost all winter.
Bears, woodchucks, lizards, frogs,
toads, turtles and some snakes
take a long winter snooze.

Did You Know?

An archer fish knocks an insect into the water by squirting it with water. Then he eats the insect.

A sponge is really an animal, even though it doesn't look like one. It gets food from sea water flowing through holes in its body.

A sea otter breaks open a clam shell by banging the shell on a rock it has brought up from the ocean floor. Then the sea otter eats the clam.

Bees dance around to show other bees where the nectar is.

Chameleons disguise themselves by changing color to match their surroundings.

African weaverbirds live in "apartment" houses. They build huge straw houses that 100 families of weaverbirds can live in together.

Twiddlebugs work all day and twiddle all night.

An elephant can hold six quarts of water in his trunk.

Prairie dogs live in prairie dog "towns." Their burrow homes are close together. The prairie dogs stand on mounds of earth around the burrows to keep watch for enemies.

37

Eyes, Ears and Noses

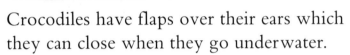

A flounder's eyes are on the top of its body. It lives at the bottom of the ocean, so it never looks down.

Crocodiles have flaps over their ears which they can close when they go underwater.

Hippopotamuses can close their nostrils underwater.

Camels and giraffes can close their nostrils when they are in sand or dust storms.

Bloodhounds can follow a scent for miles.

Grasshoppers have very large eyes made up of many small eyes. They can see in several directions at the same time.

"But only monsters have round googly eyes!"

Hard Facts About Teeth

What are fangs?

Long, pointed teeth, just like the Count's, are called fangs. Bats have fangs. Some snakes have fangs that squirt poison when the snake bites an enemy.

"Why did the bat brush his fangs?"

"Because he didn't want to have bat breath."

Do animals brush their teeth?

No, but some animals have their teeth cleaned for them. Little fish nibble food from between sharks' teeth and small birds pick crocodiles' teeth clean. When dogs chew on bones their teeth get cleaned.

Do sharks lose their teeth?

Yes. Most sharks have five or six rows of teeth. When a tooth in the first row is broken or lost one from the second row moves up and takes its place. Some sharks grow a new row of teeth every two weeks.

"The shark tooth fairy must be very busy!"

SHARK'S TEETH

Hard Facts About Bones

Not all animals have bones.
Jellyfish don't have bones. Neither do
worms, spiders or insects.

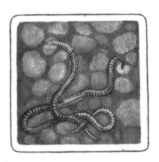  

Do birds have bones?
Yes. One reason birds can fly is that
their bones are very light and filled with
pockets of air.

BIRD

ANATOSAURUS
(DUCK-BILLED DINOSAUR)
NO. AMERICA

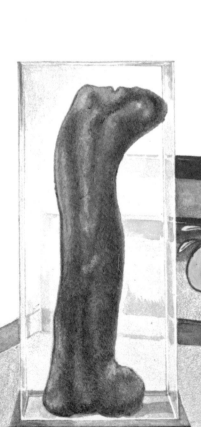

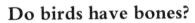

DINOSAUR THIGH BONE

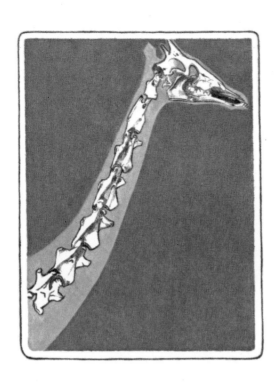

A giraffe has seven bones in its neck.
A sparrow has fourteen bones in its neck.

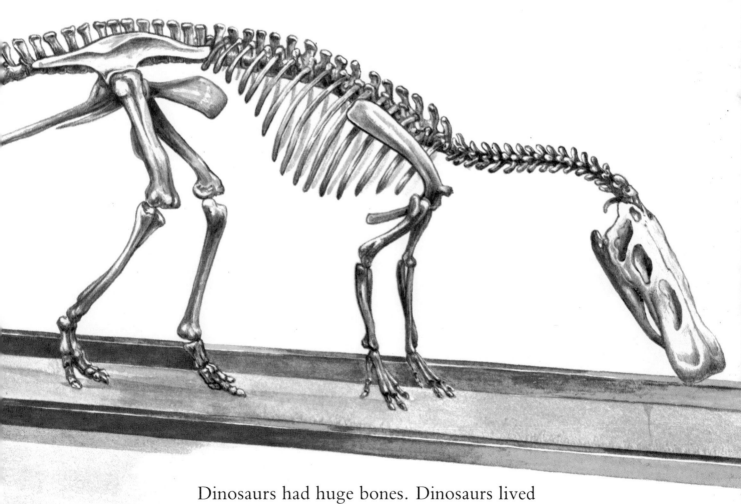

Dinosaurs had huge bones. Dinosaurs lived
millions of years ago and all that is left of them
is their bones.

Have You Heard?

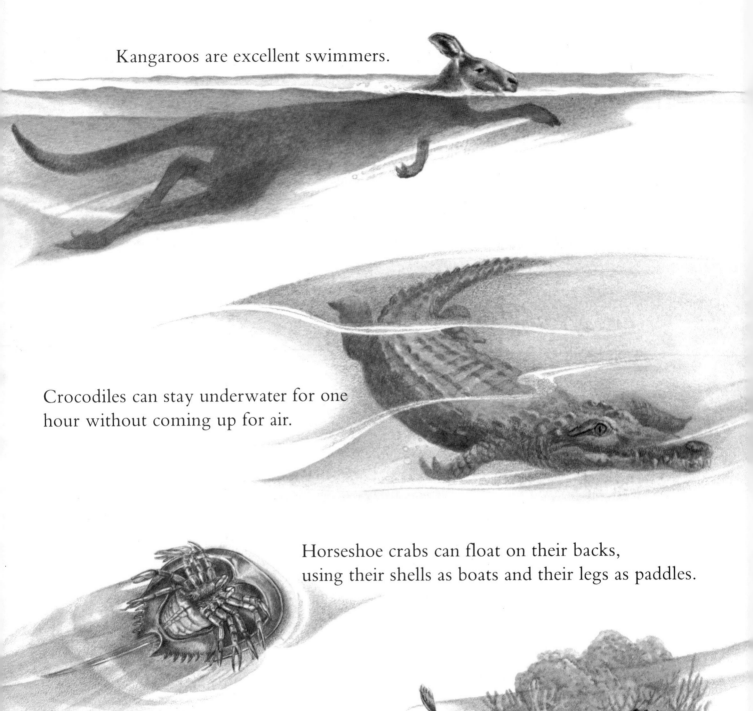

Kangaroos are excellent swimmers.

Crocodiles can stay underwater for one hour without coming up for air.

Horseshoe crabs can float on their backs, using their shells as boats and their legs as paddles.

Batfish crawl along the bottom of the ocean instead of swimming.

Gorillas make nests in trees just like
birds. But gorillas don't lay eggs
in their nests; they sleep in them.

Seashells are the hard outer covering of some
sea animals. When the animals die, their shells
may be washed onto the shore.

Lantern fish live where it's dark
and they can make their own light.

"That is so they can see in
the middle of the night
when they get up for
a glass of water."

The Tail End

How do animals use their tails?

Beavers use their tails to pack down mud on their dams.

Beavers slap their tails on the water to warn other beavers of danger.

Kangaroos use their tails to push themselves off the ground when they jump.

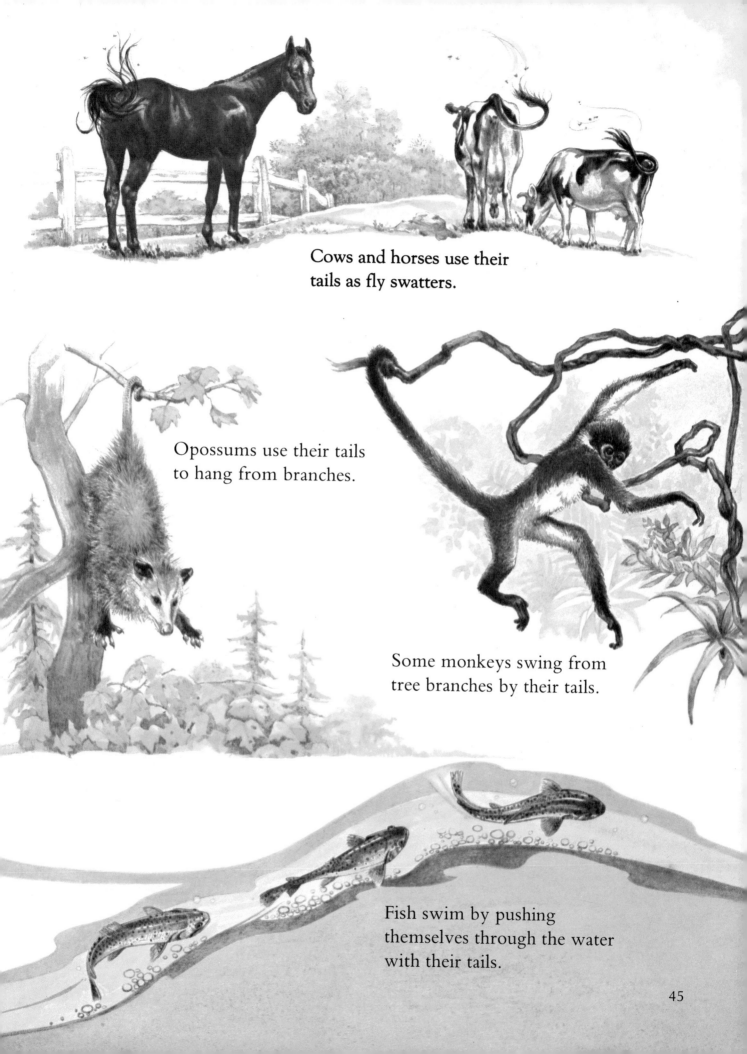

Cows and horses use their tails as fly swatters.

Opossums use their tails to hang from branches.

Some monkeys swing from tree branches by their tails.

Fish swim by pushing themselves through the water with their tails.

45